4

Chapter One: Seen it on TV

9

Chapter Two: 999!

14

**Chapter Three:
The Training Partner**

19

Chapter Four: Broke

23

Chapter Five: The Toughest Time

30

Chapter Six: The Trials

35

Chapter Seven: 2012 Olympics

41

**Chapter Eight: Making
History... Again**

Chapter One:

Seen it on TV

Nicola and her younger brother, Kurtis, were in the lounge watching TV.

Suddenly, their mum burst in. "Come on, you two. Get your coats on. The

babysitter is ill. You're going to have
to come with me to the sports centre."

At the sports centre, Nicola's mum went
off to her aerobics class, while Kurtis
quickly found his way to the football
pitch. A sports coach came over to Nicola.

"What about you, young lady?" he
asked. "What would you like to have
a go at? Maybe a dance class?"

Nicola frowned and shook her head.
"I want to do boxing," she said.

"Boxing?" the coach repeated with a snort. "You're a girl! Girls don't box..." Then he saw the determined look on Nicola's face. He knew straight away it would be no good arguing with her.

"OK," the coach sighed. "This way. Come and find me when you've had enough."

The rest of the boxing group were all boys. Nicola wasn't surprised. She didn't mind either. When it came to her turn to put on the gloves, none of the boys could land a punch near her.

At the end of the session the boxing instructor took Nicola to one side. "You seemed to know what you were doing there," he said. "How come?"

Nicola shrugged. "I've seen it on TV," she explained. "When I was little and my dad looked after us, he'd put on

these videos of old boxing matches.
His favourite was called 'Rumble in the
Jungle'."

The boxing instructor grinned. "That's a
famous fight, that one. Muhammad Ali
versus George Foreman."

Nicola nodded. "But my favourite video was of Joe Frazier denting his punch bag with his fists." She smiled at the memory of watching it with her dad. She'd only been about eight or nine, but she had realised, even then, that she had a dream: a dream to become a top boxer.

Chapter Two:
999!

Leroy Brown, trainer at the Burmantofts
Amateur Boxing Club in Leeds, stared
at Nicola long and hard. The guys at
the sports centre had said she was "a
natural".

"You're too young," he said.

"I'm twelve," answered Nicola, crossly.

"Yeah, but you're a girl. Girls don't box," he said.

"This one does," replied Nicola, quick as a flash.

Leroy sighed. "Well, I suppose there's no harm in letting you have a go against some of the lads here. But you'll be the only girl here."

Nicola shrugged.

Nicola boxed at the Burmantofts Amateur Boxing Club week in, week out. At home, her mum and dad were splitting up and things were tough. The boxing club gave her a chance to get away from all the unhappiness.

About a year after she'd joined the club, when she was thirteen, Nicola persuaded Leroy to let her fight her first competitive bout. She won it easily.

"Can you fix me up with another match?" she asked Leroy.

"I'd love to," he said. "But it's not going to be easy, finding someone who can give you a decent match. You're good."

Nicola ran home, feeling on top of the world. Deep down, she'd always known that she was a good boxer. To have an experienced coach like Leroy actually tell her so was a bit special.

She got home to the flat and raced through to the kitchen. There was no one there. Straight away Nicola sensed that something was wrong. Her mum was always in the kitchen when she got back from boxing, waiting to hear how she had got on.

Nicola heard a noise coming from her mum's bedroom. She ran through and saw her mum lying on the bedroom floor. She was breathing heavily. There were beads of sweat on her forehead. Her eyes were glazed and she was mumbling.

Nicola dialled 999.

Chapter Three:

The Training Partner

Nicola's mum had meningitis, a very serious illness that can be fatal. While her mum was ill, Nicola had to do all the cleaning and washing, and look after her younger brother, Kurtis. All the time, she was worried that her mum might die.

Gradually though, her mum got better and Nicola was able to go back to the boxing club. As always, she enjoyed sparring with the boys, but her coach Leroy still couldn't find another girl boxer for Nicola to fight in a competitive bout.

In fact, Nicola was seventeen before she had her second proper match. She'd had to wait four years! This time the match was even shorter than her first one. Nicola was declared the winner in round two after she knocked her opponent down.

Every week, Nicola asked Leroy to try to find her a sparring partner who would really test her boxing skills.

Leroy just sighed and shook his head sadly. "I just don't know who would be tough enough, Nicola. But one thing's for sure, if you're going to reach the top of the game, you'll need some tougher workouts than you're getting with the lads here."

Then one day, Leroy called Nicola over to his office. "I've found another boxer for you to train with," he said. "I think he'll be somebody who can help you raise your game."

"Is he any good?" asked Nicola, doubtfully.

"I'd say he's more than good," replied Leroy, with a grin. "You might have heard of him. His name's David Haye."

Nicola gave Leroy a suspicious look.
"This is a wind-up, right?"

Leroy held up his hands. "No, I'm
serious. He's heard all about you and
is looking forward to working with you
as your new training partner. Good
news, eh?"

"You bet," said Nicola, excitedly.

She had every right to be excited. David
Haye had just taken the heavyweight
silver medal at the 2001 World Amateur
Boxing Championships. He was one of
the top boxers in Britain.

Chapter Four:
Broke

Training with a successful boxer near the top of his game was just what Nicola needed. She and David got on well. "You're good," he told her.

"You mean I'm good for a girl?" replied Nicola with a frown.

"No," David answered. "I mean you're good. And you can get better. Just work hard and aim high."

Nicola took David's advice. In 2001 she became the first woman to represent England at an international boxing tournament.

Just two years later, aged nineteen, Nicola travelled to the Croft Gymnasium at the Metropolitan Police College in London. She was fighting in the first-ever women's English National Amateur Boxing Championships. Nicola finished as the tournament champion. She remained champion for four years.

The more Nicola boxed, the more it cost her for training, travel and equipment. She was broke and her mum didn't have much money, either.

"I'm four-times English champion," she sighed. "Surely someone will sponsor me and help pay for me to fight?"

But no one did. Sports sponsors didn't want to know about helping a woman boxer. So to pay her way, Nicola took jobs on building sites as a painter and decorator. She acted as an extra in *Coronation Street* and *Emmerdale*.

Nicola's mum tried to help her out, too. But times were hard.

Leroy reminded her, "What you've got to remember is that it was only in 1996 that the Amateur Boxing Association lifted its ban on women's boxing. That ban had been in place for over a hundred years. But now, there are more than half a million licensed women boxers across the world. Take it from me, women's boxing is gaining support."

Leroy was right. But what neither he nor Nicola knew was that women's boxing was about to receive a massive boost.

Chapter Five:

The Toughest Time

In August 2009, the International Olympic Committee met in Berlin, Germany. They were there to decide whether any new sports should be added to the next Olympic Games.

At the end of the meeting, the International Olympic Committee president, Jacques Rogge, held a press conference.

"Added to women's sports to be featured at the 2012 London Games," he announced, "will be boxing."

There was a buzz of excitement amongst the gathered journalists.

"Until now," Jacques Rogge went on, "boxing has been the only Olympic sport with no women included. The sport has progressed a lot in the last five years and it is about time we included it in the games." Women's boxing had last featured in the Olympic Games in 1904. But it had been an exhibition event only: no medals were awarded.

Nicola was thrilled. Because women's boxing was now an Olympic sport, she

got some sponsorship, including a car, so that she could travel to fights and the gym more easily.

"Looks like you're set up," Leroy said. "Train hard, and you'll be in with a good chance at the Olympic trials."

Nicola began to put in extra hours' training. One day, she was in her room listening to music when her mum called up the stairs, "Nicola! Hurry up! You'll be late!"

Nicola looked at her watch. She suddenly remembered she'd planned to go to the gym early. She grabbed her coat and bag and rushed out of the flat. Halfway down the steps she tripped and fell. When she landed at the bottom her back hurt like mad. Nicola struggled to

get up, but somehow she made it
to the gym and carried on training
and sparring.

A few days later though, the pain in her back was so bad she couldn't get out of bed. She went to hospital for X-rays.

The doctor put the X-rays up on the screen for Nicola to see. "You've broken a bone in your back," she said. "It means at least three months in bed."

It was the toughest time Nicola had ever faced as a boxer. Up and down the country women boxers were taking part in tryouts: the first stage in securing a place in the women's boxing team for the Olympic Games. All she could do was lie on her back all day with only her Doberman puppy, Dexter, for company. She couldn't see how she'd ever be able to box again.

Chapter Six:
The Trials

By the time the very last Olympic trials were taking place, Nicola was out of bed. She was still in a lot of pain though.

"What are you going to do?" Nicola's mum asked her as they sat down together at the kitchen table.

"I'll go to the Olympic trials," said
Nicola, "and see how I get on."

At the trials Nicola was still in a lot
of pain and her movements were
restricted. Somehow, though, she
managed to get through all the bouts.

For two days afterwards, Nicola couldn't move at all. She was worried she had made her back injury worse, but gradually, the pain eased and she was able to start walking again.

Later that week Nicola's phone rang — she didn't recognise the number.

"Hello?"

"Is that Nicola Adams?"

"Yes..?"

"I've got some good news for you. Provided your recovery continues to go well we'd like you to join Team GB's women's boxing squad for the London Olympics."

Nicola rushed through to the kitchen to tell her mum the good news.

"I knew you could do it, girl!" her mum cried, giving Nicola a big hug.

"Ow, careful, Mum! Don't hug me so tight! You're hurting my back," laughed Nicola.

Sensing that something exciting was happening, Dexter barked loudly from the doorway.

Once the excitement of getting a place in Team GB was over, the hard work of preparing for an Olympic Games began. Nicola's training schedule got tougher. All around the world, boxers were training for the games too, and she found the competition was getting tougher.

In 2010, she competed in the Women's World Championships. She won silver, losing to the Chinese boxer Ren Cancan in the final. She lost again to Ren

Cancan at the 2012 Women's World Championships.

Nicola was well aware that the Olympics was a world competition too. She knew she would need to beat the likes of Ren Cancan to be in with a chance of a medal.

34

Chapter Seven:

2012 Olympics

On a bright July morning in 2012, Nicola took Dexter to the kennels and said goodbye to him before heading off to the Olympic village in London.

Famous athletes from all over the world were gathering for the world's biggest sporting event. There was a real buzz of excitement! Nicola blended into the team; she wasn't famous and women's boxing was still a minority sport. The team coach thought that she might pick up a medal, but at some stage she would have to face the reigning world champion, Ren Cancan, again.

The qualifying rounds went well for Nicola. In the semi-finals she faced the Indian boxer Mary Kom, a five-time world champion. Nicola beat her 11 points to 6. Now came her greatest test: the final against the toughest opponent of all, Ren Cancan.

Nicola started the bout quietly, but took the first round 4 points to 2. Then, in round two she landed a left to Ren Cancan's chin, quickly followed by a right. Ren lost her balance and staggered backwards onto the canvas.

When the round restarted, another accurate jab unsettled Ren Cancan again. Nicola was full of confidence now, dancing away from Ren Cancan's increasingly desperate punches. The home crowd was going mad with excitement. Nicola's mum and family, her coach and trainers were there too, cheering her on.

In the final round, Nicola finished the fight with a flourish: a massive left hook of which the great Muhammad Ali would have been proud.

At the end of the bout, the judges declared Nicola the winner, 16 points to 7.

Nicola had become the first woman in history to win an Olympic medal for boxing.

When she stepped down from the

winners' podium, she was surrounded by cameras and journalists.

"How are you going to celebrate your win, Nicola?" one of them asked her.

"I'm going down Nando's for a chicken pitta medium with chips. Then I'm going home to take Dexter for a walk," replied Nicola, with a grin.

Chapter Eight:

Making History... Again

Nicola's triumph at the Olympic Games propelled her to fame. Letter boxes in her home town — Leeds — were painted gold in honour of her gold medal win. In 2013 she was appointed MBE in the New Year Honours list.

In 2014, Nicola faced her next big competition: the Commonwealth Games in Glasgow. She couldn't help thinking how different things were now compared to the Olympic Games two years before. Then, she was an unknown. Now, she was Olympic champion and everyone expected her to take gold at the Commonwealth Games, too.

Just as she had at the Olympic Games, Nicola sailed easily through the qualifying rounds. Her opponent in the final was to be the young Northern Irish boxer, Michaela Walsh.

The first round was close. Nicola realised that her opponent was less nervous and more fired up than Ren Cancan had been at the Olympics. The second round went to Nicola, but the third and fourth rounds were both very close. In every round Nicola fought hard

to get in the first and last punches of each exchange. It was something she knew would count in her favour when the judges scored the fight.

At the end of the bout, both boxers stood with the referee. They waited for the judges' decision, knowing it had been a close fight. Eventually, the judges announced that Nicola had won the bout on a split decision.

Nicola punched the air in celebration — she felt so proud! As a small girl, all those years ago, she had been inspired by videos of boxing greats Muhammad Ali and Joe Frazier to dream to win matches as a top boxer.

Now she had won the first-ever women's boxing Commonwealth gold.

And once again, she had created sporting history.

DREAM TO WIN

Fact file
Nicola Adams

Full name: Nicola Adams

Born: 26 October 1982, Leeds, England

Height: 1.65 metres

Medals
— 2007 European Amateur Championships (Velje, Denmark)
Silver, Bantamweight — the first Englishwoman to win a medal in a major boxing tournament

— 2008 World Amateur Championships (Ningbo, China)
Silver, Bantamweight

— 2010 World Amateur Championships (Bridgeton, Barbados)
Silver, Flyweight

— 2011 European Union Amateur Championships (Katowice, Poland)
Gold, Flyweight

— 2011 European Amateur Championships (Rotterdam, Holland)
Gold, Flyweight

— 2012 Olympic Games (London, UK)
Gold — Flyweight
The first woman to become an Olympic boxing champion

— 2013 European Union Amateur Championships (Keszthely, Hungary)
Gold — Flyweight

— 2014 Commonwealth Games (Glasgow, Scotland)
Gold — Flyweight — the first woman to become a Commonwealth Games boxing champion

Other achievements
— 2001 Became the first woman to represent England at boxing

— 2003, 2004, 2005, 2006 England women's amateur boxing champion

Other honours:
— 2012 Joe Bromley Award for Outstanding Service to Boxing

— 2013 Appointed Member of the Order of the British Empire [MBE]

Louis Smith

"So, you've brought Louis to be auditioned for the cathedral choir?" asked the man behind the piano. He could see Louis fidgeting and looking bored. "Well, I suppose I'd better hear him sing."

So Louis sang.

When he had finished, Louis' mum turned to the man behind the piano and said, "What do you think, then?"

The man slowly smiled. "I think Louis has a most wonderful voice. I'd be delighted to offer him a place in the cathedral choir."

Continue reading this story in:
DREAM TO WIN:
Louis Smith